FEELING SENS
BEING A HIGHLY SENSITIVE KID

By Tracy Bryan

"It is my belief that this trait is a special gift because it opens you up to a wide world of amazing possibilities and potentials."

-Jim Hallowes
Adapted from
highlysensitivepeople.com

FEELING SENSITIVE!
BEING A HIGHLY SENSITIVE KID

By Tracy Bryan

Are there times when you feel overly sensitive to your surroundings?

You feel so sensitive and you get easily overwhelmed from certain people or situations that upset you?

You feel so sensitive and you can't seem to clear your head or calm your body when this happens?

You feel so sensitive and you want to run away from whatever it is that is making you feel this way?

This is totally normal and actually kind of common!
In fact, research shows that 15-20% of the population has a high sensory processing trait in their personality.[1]

A special psychotherapist, named Dr. Elaine Aron, has done a lot of research studying people with this personality trait. She calls a person with this trait a Highly Sensitive Person or HSP.

When compared to most people, a Highly Sensitive Person or HSP is best described as someone who:

1. feels more deeply
2. has more awareness with their senses (sight, sound, touch, taste, feel)
3. reacts more emotionally to people and situations
4. likes time alone and is comfortable being alone
5. may be shy
6. takes longer to make decisions
7. pays attention to details
8. cries more easily
9. is sensitive to criticism
10. shows more empathy for others than most people [2]

HSPs have many positive characteristics that are part of their sensitivity. It's important to look at all the characteristics in order to understand WHY HSPs are the way they are.

Anyone with any condition is just as awesome as anyone else. Some people just have to work a little bit harder in certain ways. They are not weaker, they just function differently and more uniquely than most people.

Everybody's mind and body functions in a certain way. When someone has a condition, this disrupts the way these work. If the mind and body don't function properly, this causes a problem. People that are highly sensitive have a problem functioning like everybody else, because of their sensitivity. They have to work a little harder than most people at coping with their sensitivity when they process their surroundings.

Everybody's mind and body has to PROCESS their surroundings in everyday life. We process with all our senses- sight, sound, touch, taste and feel. We process everything around us- other people, places, things and situations. Sometimes processing all this can be a little bit more difficult for HSPs because of all the characteristics in their condition.

This condition has a scientific name too- Sensory Processing Sensitivity.(3) This basically means; people with this condition feel their senses (sight, sound, touch, taste and feel) more intensely when they process their surroundings.

It's important to look at all the characteristics of Sensory Processing Sensitivity in order to understand WHAT someone with this condition feels.

Studies show that Highly Sensitive People feel more deeply than most people and like to process things on a deeper level. They're very intuitive, and think more to try and figure things out.(4) HSPs can be very intuitive because they have a sharp awareness of their senses and notice more smells, sights, sounds, tastes and have more feelings than most people.

A Highly Sensitive Person is born with a nervous system that is highly aware and quick to react to everything. HSPs are incredibly responsive to the people and situations they experience.(5)

When something stressful happens to any of us, we naturally try to REACT to it. We usually react to situations that are unfamiliar to us, make us feel uncomfortable, upset us or situations that we fear. Instead of processing these situations for a little bit longer, and then calmly RESPONDING to these situations, most people will instantly react to them.

We react this way because ALL people feel the need to instinctively protect themselves from any thing, person or situation that threatens them- anything uncomfortable, painful, stressful or scary. We will do just about anything to avoid any one of these conditions.

Having this feeling towards any of these threatening conditions is our body's instinctive way of protecting itself from danger.

Every human since the beginning of time has had this need to protect themselves from danger. This is called the FIGHT OR FLIGHT RESPONSE. Here's how it works-

Imagine you're a caveman or cavewoman living 100,000 years ago - and you come face to face with a hungry saber-toothed tiger. You have two choices: 1) Run for it (that's flight), or 2) pick up your club and battle the tiger (that's fight). A final choice (be eaten) doesn't seem like such a good one!

To prepare for fight or flight, your body does a number of things automatically so it's ready for quick action or a quick escape. Your heart rate increases to pump more blood to your muscles and brain. Your lungs take in air faster to supply your body with oxygen. The pupils in your eyes get larger to see better. And your digestive and urinary systems slow down for the moment so you can concentrate on more important things.[6]

Highly Sensitive People have a strong sense of awareness and so they feel the Fight or Flight Response that much more intensely. HSPs may feel uncomfortable in situations where other people don't and they may sense danger when others are not even aware of it.

This is mainly because the brain of a Highly Sensitive person processes information and reflects on it more deeply than most people. (7) Sometimes, when they feel the Fight or Flight Response, HSPs have an intense need to protect themselves.

The good news is that HSPs also feel empathy and compassion more intensely too, not only fear. Just as they would react to unsafe situations, they also react to situations where kindness for others is needed.

People who are highly sensitive will react more emotionally in most situations. As an example-they will have empathy and feel more concern for a friend's problems because they are in tune to what other people are feeling too. (8)

HSPs are often gifted intellectually, creatively and emotionally, demonstrating genuine compassion at early ages. The downside is that as adults and kids, these intensely perceptive people can also get overwhelmed easily by crowds, noises, new situations, sudden changes and the emotional distress of others. (9)

Most Highly Sensitive People prefer spaces where they aren't overly stimulated, because of their tendency to overreact in more stressful situations and places.

In kids that are highly sensitive, sometimes this overreaction causes them to behave in ways that some people may not be able to understand at first.

They may complain about something that wouldn't bother most kids. They may not like the texture or taste of a food being served. Or, they may get upset by the itchy fabric on their clothes. Physical complaints are common in these kids because this is their body's natural reaction to the stress of overstimulation. (10)

During any uncomfortable, stressful or frightening situation that any of us have to go through, it helps to know some simple MINDFULNESS coping skills to get through them.

Mindfulness means having a moment-by-moment awareness of our thoughts, feelings, bodily sensations, and surrounding environment.

Mindfulness also involves acceptance, meaning that we pay attention to our thoughts and feelings without judging them- there's no "right" or "wrong" way to think or feel in a given moment.

When we practice mindfulness, our thoughts tune into what we're sensing in the present moment, rather than thinking about what has happened in the past or imagining what may happen in the future. (11)

When you're feeling a certain way about the situation your in and you don't like it, use your breath to change how your feeling. STOP, BREATHE, BECOME AWARE and NOTICE...

STOP what you're doing and thinking-sit down if you need to, even close your eyes if you like.

BREATHE in slowly, as deeply as you can and hold it in for a few minutes. Now let the breath out and repeat this for as long as you need to. Keep doing this until you feel calmer.

BECOME AWARE to how your body feels (imagine turning your mind off with a switch-no thinking)keep breathing!
How does your body feel? Is it restless or agitated? What do you feel in your legs, arms and belly? Does your body feel hungry or thirsty? Can you feel any vibrations running through your body?

NOTICE the way your body feels...hopefully it's calmer now. Hopefully it feels less sensitive!

When we clear our mind and calm our body by breathing mindfully, it's a lot easier to cope with challenging situations that we are afraid of. Mindful breathing really helps us cope with our feelings, so we can RESPOND to places, people, and all situations that we have to face. This is the basics of mindfulness practice.

People who have Sensory Processing Sensitivity may have to use this coping skill a little bit more than most people, but they're actually really good at it, because HSPs have a natural ability to NOTICE. They notice what is going on around them really well and noticing is an extremely important part of this mindful breathing skill!

HSPs are highly sensitive, highly mindful, highly creative and highly processing of their senses. HSPs have so many awesome characteristics in their personality.

Are you a HSP? Are you...

Feeling Sensitive?

Glossary

Awareness-the state or condition of being aware

Characteristics-special features

Compassion-a feeling of deep sympathy and sorrow for another person

Condition-a medical state of being

Diaphragmatic Breathing-abdominal breathing that engages the diaphragm, (that big muscle shaped like a boomerang just under your lungs), to expand the belly as the lungs fill completely and deeply with air.

Empathy-the ability to understand the feelings of another person

Fight or Flight Response-humans natural reaction to danger or fear

Function-a system of how something/someone works

Nervous System-the system of nerves and nerve centers in an animal or human (ie. the brain, spinal cord, nerves)

Process-a series of actions

React-to act instantly

Respond-to reply in action

Sensitivity-the state of being sensitive

Sensory Processing-the system of using the senses

Stimulate-to rouse to action

Tendency-having the intention to move

6 Quick Tips to Help You Deal with New Places

Visit a place before you actually have to be there so you can picture it in your head.

Take a peek around a new place so you know the lay of the land and work out the directions to where you need to be - it's one less thing to stress about.

Look at photos of a new place (e.g. a new school - make a photo book with pictures of the school exterior, the classroom, the cafeteria, the gym, the playground etc. before you have to actually start school).

Meeting your new teacher before the start of school is a good idea. Browsing their online photo may be enough so you know what they look like before you meet them.

Give yourself plenty of time to find your way to a new location, and if it makes you feel more comfortable ask someone to accompany you.

Worry less!

Adapted from happysensitivekids.wordpress.com

Relaxation Toolbox for Fear
(Mindful Breathing & Guided Meditations)

1 Take a Deep Breath:
Stop, drop and....take a deep breath. At the very first signs of fear, taking a deep breath signals the body that it's time to calm down. The deep breath, also known as diaphragmatic breathing, belly breathing and abdominal breathing is breath that engages the diaphragm, (that big muscle shaped like a boomerang just under your lungs), to expand the belly as the lungs fill completely and deeply with air.

This is a deep breath exercise called the seated cat breath that you can do in a chair, great for the classroom at school:

2 Seated Cat Breath:
Sit in a chair with your back as straight as possible and your hands on your thighs. As you breathe out, bend forward, round your back like a cat, push your chin towards your chest, and press up with your hands, emptying out your lungs until they are empty. Now breathe in, allowing your tummy to push outward filling up with air, allowing your back to arch and your chin to lift upwards, bending your head slightly backwards. Good! Now repeat the process several times, paying attention to the in and out flow of air in your lungs.

Visualization: Park Bench Friends

Close your eyes and allow your body to get comfortable. Take a deep breath in through your nose and let it out gently through your mouth. Imagine that you are sitting in a beautiful park. There might be birds chirping or maybe you can see the trees swaying with the breeze. Imagine that you find a park bench and you sit down overlooking a beautiful view. Now, invite your Fear to sit down next to you on the bench, like you would invite a friend. Good! As you are sitting there next to Fear, ask Fear what it needs right now. Listen as fear tells you what you need to know. (Pause) If any memories or thoughts come up, invite them to sit down beside you too. See them all lined up beside you on the bench. Awesome! Now ask Fear if there are any spots in your body that need more love and care, maybe where Fear likes to hang out. Good! Gently put your hand on those spots to give them some love. Now, maybe you can imagine that you have a very special camera that can give you a bigger picture of what is going on with Fear. Maybe you can allow that camera lens to widen to get that big picture. See what you see. Good! (Pause) Ask Fear if there is anything else you need to know right now. Thank Fear, give Fear a high five, or hug Fear, any way that you want to thank Fear for sitting there with you and let Fear know that everything is okay. Allow Fear to walk away and know that you can come back here any time to talk to Fear. Begin to bring your attention back to your body and the room around you. You can open your eyes when you are ready.

Adapted from kidsrelaxation.com- For many more deep breathing activities, check out the ebook called Deep Breathing For Kids by Zemirah

Essential Websites About HSP

drtedzeff.com
happysensitivekids.wordpress.com
healingtreefoundation.org
highlysensitive.org
highlysensitivepower.com
hsperson.com
hsphealth.com
kidsrelaxation.com
sensitiveandextraordinary.com

To find out if you may be a HSP, please visit the following
link with your parents and take the test:

hsperson.com/test/highly-sensitive-test/

Resources

(1) hsperson.com/research
(2) huffingtonpost.com
(3) hsperson.com
(4) Dr. Ted Zeff, Ph.D., author of The Highly Sensitive Person's Survival Guide
(5) psychologytoday.com
(6) kidshealth.org
(7) hsperson.com
(8) huffingtonpost.com
(9) psychologytoday.com
(10) healingtreefoundation.org
(11) greatergood.berkeley.edu

A Message From The Author...

Just lately I figured out that I was a HSP. I always kind of knew though that something was different about the way that I processed and used my senses so intensely in my life. Instead of calling myself different, I like to use the word UNIQUE! I am unique and so are you- everyone is actually, but HSPs are even that much more unique because of all the cool characteristics that we have in our personality. It's important to remember this when you have to cope with situations that may be difficult for you...just breathe-you'll get through it! Good Luck!
Trace:)

A Special Dedication To...
Nancy

Thank you for introducing this personality trait to me. Thank you for helping me see just how wonderful my authentic self can be. Thank you for sharing tips on coping with being an introvert and helping me see this part of myself that was hiding. Thank you for finding a path for me to take and gently urging me on my way to a new life. Most of all, thank you for loving me and making me feel safe so I could just come out and play.

Love Me:)

Tracy's Reading Recommendations...

If you like this book, check out another book in my Being Awesome! Series:

Being You! Daily Mindfulness For Kids

There are so many ways that we can practice loving ourselves. Each day, there are little things that we can do to remind ourselves just how great we really are.

From morning to night, follow along in this book and practice ways to love yourself.

Learn tools to deal with people who make you feel bad. Face uncomfortable situations. Understand about mindfulness and why it helps you manage your feelings. Discover a YOU that is totally fantastic!

Totally Mindful!

Look forward to reading with you:)

Made in the USA
Monee, IL
04 May 2024

57960147R00033